The Funny Side of Hunting and Fishing

A Cartoonist's Guide to the Sports of the Great Outdoors

By

Daniel Roberts

All titles, characters and their likenesses are
property of their respective owners

© 2003 by Daniel Roberts. All rights reserved.

No part of this book may be reproduced, stored in a retrieval system, or transmitted by any means, electronic, mechanical, photocopying, recording, or otherwise, without written permission from the author.

ISBN: 1-4107-0768-7 (e-book)
ISBN: 1-4107-0769-5 (Paperback)

Library of Congress Control Number: 2002096845

This book is printed on acid free paper.

Printed in the United States of America
Bloomington, IN

1stBooks – rev. 3/7/03

For all those who have supported, encouraged, and believed in my artwork.

Table of Contents

The Funny Side of Deer Hunting 1

The Funny Side of Duck Hunting 59

The Funny Side of Hunters 68

The Funny Side of Fishing 80

The Funny Side of Hunting and Fishing
A Cartoonist's Guide to the Sports of the Great Outdoors

The Funny Side of Deer Hunting

Daniel Roberts

The Funny Side of Hunting and Fishing
A Cartoonist's Guide to the Sports of the Great Outdoors

"WHIPLASH! WHIPLASH! SOMEONE CALL MY LAWYER!"

Daniel Roberts

"I think he knows we're out of ammo!"

The Funny Side of Hunting and Fishing
A Cartoonist's Guide to the Sports of the Great Outdoors

Daniel Roberts

"Who's the wise guy?!?!"

The Funny Side of Hunting and Fishing
A Cartoonist's Guide to the Sports of the Great Outdoors

"Never a dry eye in the house!"

Daniel Roberts

"I haven't seen any signs telling me it's hunting season."

The Funny Side of Hunting and Fishing
A Cartoonist's Guide to the Sports of the Great Outdoors

Daniel Roberts

"PEEK-A-BOO! I SEE YOU!"

The Funny Side of Hunting and Fishing
A Cartoonist's Guide to the Sports of the Great Outdoors

"Of all the things Mrs. Claus could have given him for Christmas last year, why'd she'd give him a bow hunting set!"

Daniel Roberts

"I'll be with you in a moment."

The Funny Side of Hunting and Fishing
A Cartoonist's Guide to the Sports of the Great Outdoors

Daniel Roberts

"Could you come back latter? I'm on my smoke break."

The Funny Side of Hunting and Fishing
A Cartoonist's Guide to the Sports of the Great Outdoors

"What do you mean I don't qualify for disablity? I've got a BAD BACK!"

Daniel Roberts

"I take it you forgot your hunting license but remembered your wedding license."

The Funny Side of Hunting and Fishing
A Cartoonist's Guide to the Sports of the Great Outdoors

"Could you hurry up? I don't have all day!"

Daniel Roberts

"Just wait til the next hunter messes with us...
WHAM!"

The Funny Side of Hunting and Fishing
A Cartoonist's Guide to the Sports of the Great Outdoors

Daniel Roberts

"Interesting trophy."

*The Funny Side of Hunting and Fishing
A Cartoonist's Guide to the Sports of the Great Outdoors*

"Sorry. We don't have any bullets on us either."

Daniel Roberts

The Funny Side of Hunting and Fishing
A Cartoonist's Guide to the Sports of the Great Outdoors

Daniel Roberts

"No I.D.. I'm afraid we'll have to mark her down as a Jane DOE."

The Funny Side of Hunting and Fishing
A Cartoonist's Guide to the Sports of the Great Outdoors

"I'm really getting close."

Daniel Roberts

"He must be a vegetarian."

The Funny Side of Hunting and Fishing
A Cartoonist's Guide to the Sports of the Great Outdoors

"Rats! Got them mixed up again!"

Daniel Roberts

"Remember to wipe your feet the next time!"

The Funny Side of Hunting and Fishing
A Cartoonist's Guide to the Sports of the Great Outdoors

"There I was, looking down the barrel of his gun when suddenly... it backfired!"

Daniel Roberts

"Next year we pick out your Christmas present!"

*The Funny Side of Hunting and Fishing
A Cartoonist's Guide to the Sports of the Great Outdoors*

"And the goal is good!"

Daniel Roberts

"We'll have to come back another time. We ran out of beer!"

The Funny Side of Hunting and Fishing
A Cartoonist's Guide to the Sports of the Great Outdoors

"This is the first time you've bow hunted, isn't it?"

Daniel Roberts

"I kill more deer this way than I do when I'm hunting."

The Funny Side of Hunting and Fishing
A Cartoonist's Guide to the Sports of the Great Outdoors

"I hope my insurance covers this."

Daniel Roberts

"Now the odds are a little more even!"

The Funny Side of Hunting and Fishing
A Cartoonist's Guide to the Sports of the Great Outdoors

"My doctor says that hunting is bad for my health."

Daniel Roberts

"Why is it I'm the one stuck doing all the work?"

The Funny Side of Hunting and Fishing
A Cartoonist's Guide to the Sports of the Great Outdoors

Daniel Roberts

"This isn't what I was expecting when you said you were bringing deer home for supper."

*The Funny Side of Hunting and Fishing
A Cartoonist's Guide to the Sports of the Great Outdoors*

"DON'T SHOOT! MY WALLET'S IN MY BACK POCKET!"

Daniel Roberts

"Can you get me a glass of water? I'm thirsty."

The Funny Side of Hunting and Fishing
A Cartoonist's Guide to the Sports of the Great Outdoors

"Shhhh! He'll hear you."

Daniel Roberts

The Funny Side of Hunting and Fishing
A Cartoonist's Guide to the Sports of the Great Outdoors

"If we wait by this sign long enough, one's bound to come by!"

Daniel Roberts

"Hey! I think I hear a deer now!"

The Funny Side of Hunting and Fishing
A Cartoonist's Guide to the Sports of the Great Outdoors

"Did you see that hunter that was after Barney the other day? Was he drunk or what?"

Daniel Roberts

"Why do they always show up when we're fishing instead of hunting?"

The Funny Side of Hunting and Fishing
A Cartoonist's Guide to the Sports of the Great Outdoors

"Next time don't forget to take the keys out of the ignition."

Daniel Roberts

"But I'm not a deer, I'm a bunny."

The Funny Side of Hunting and Fishing
A Cartoonist's Guide to the Sports of the Great Outdoors

"I took 'em out of one of those hunter's trucks!"

Daniel Roberts

"I'm erasing the evidence that we were even here."

The Funny Side of Hunting and Fishing
A Cartoonist's Guide to the Sports of the Great Outdoors

"Did you lose these?"

Daniel Roberts

"Are you done borrowing them yet?"

The Funny Side of Hunting and Fishing
A Cartoonist's Guide to the Sports of the Great Outdoors

"No wonder they call this a freezer. IT'S FREEZING IN HERE!"

Daniel Roberts

"We're not hunting that kind of DEER!"

The Funny Side of Hunting and Fishing
A Cartoonist's Guide to the Sports of the Great Outdoors

Daniel Roberts

The Funny Side of Hunting and Fishing
A Cartoonist's Guide to the Sports of the Great Outdoors

The Funny Side of Duck Hunting

Daniel Roberts

"We're after ducks. Not fish."

*The Funny Side of Hunting and Fishing
A Cartoonist's Guide to the Sports of the Great Outdoors*

"You're suppose to be after game."

Daniel Roberts

"I'm glad you take bribes!"

The Funny Side of Hunting and Fishing
A Cartoonist's Guide to the Sports of the Great Outdoors

Daniel Roberts

The Funny Side of Hunting and Fishing
A Cartoonist's Guide to the Sports of the Great Outdoors

"The duck! THE DUCK! Not the DECOY!"

Daniel Roberts

"Which one should I shoot? WHICH ONE SHOULD I SHOOT?"

The Funny Side of Hunting and Fishing
A Cartoonist's Guide to the Sports of the Great Outdoors

"I couldn't find my decoy so I'm using my rubber ducky."

Daniel Roberts

The Funny Side of Hunters

The Funny Side of Hunting and Fishing
A Cartoonist's Guide to the Sports of the Great Outdoors

Daniel Roberts

"Which of you ordered the pizza?"

*The Funny Side of Hunting and Fishing
A Cartoonist's Guide to the Sports of the Great Outdoors*

"This trap works."

Daniel Roberts

"You may not have caught anything but you did end up on television!"

The Funny Side of Hunting and Fishing
A Cartoonist's Guide to the Sports of the Great Outdoors

Daniel Roberts

The Funny Side of Hunting and Fishing
A Cartoonist's Guide to the Sports of the Great Outdoors

"OOPS!"

Daniel Roberts

"The arrow store must be that way."

The Funny Side of Hunting and Fishing
A Cartoonist's Guide to the Sports of the Great Outdoors

"All right! I put on deodarant. Now you should be able to smell something other than me!"

Daniel Roberts

"I don't own a bird DOG."

The Funny Side of Hunting and Fishing
A Cartoonist's Guide to the Sports of the Great Outdoors

"If only you could find game and as well as you can find sales."

Daniel Roberts

The Funny Side of Fishing

The Funny Side of Hunting and Fishing
A Cartoonist's Guide to the Sports of the Great Outdoors

Daniel Roberts

"I just love fresh fish."

*The Funny Side of Hunting and Fishing
A Cartoonist's Guide to the Sports of the Great Outdoors*

Daniel Roberts

"Could you take your feet out of the water? The odar's killing the fish!"

Daniel Roberts

*The Funny Side of Hunting and Fishing
A Cartoonist's Guide to the Sports of the Great Outdoors*

"I take it you didn't catch anything."

Daniel Roberts

"I knew learning to tie a knot would come in handy some day."

*The Funny Side of Hunting and Fishing
A Cartoonist's Guide to the Sports of the Great Outdoors*

""Can I have my tire back? My car wouldn't go very far without it."

Daniel Roberts

"The last time I went fishing I caught someone's HUSBAND!"

The Funny Side of Hunting and Fishing
A Cartoonist's Guide to the Sports of the Great Outdoors

"What kind of bait are YOU using?"

Daniel Roberts

"I must have caught this one right out of a school of fish."

The Funny Side of Hunting and Fishing
A Cartoonist's Guide to the Sports of the Great Outdoors

"You always have the BETTER luck!"

Daniel Roberts

*The Funny Side of Hunting and Fishing
A Cartoonist's Guide to the Sports of the Great Outdoors*

"There is a slight difference between hunting and fishing."

Daniel Roberts

"Don't I at least get a last request?"

The Funny Side of Hunting and Fishing
A Cartoonist's Guide to the Sports of the Great Outdoors

"You remember those stories about a sea monster?"

"Santa must be trying his hand at fishing again."

The Funny Side of Hunting and Fishing
A Cartoonist's Guide to the Sports of the Great Outdoors

"Must be a fisherman with a sense of humor."

Daniel Roberts

"That's not a big mouth bass. That's my wife."

Daniel Roberts

"All you have to do is reach in, grab a box of fish sticks and take it out."

*The Funny Side of Hunting and Fishing
A Cartoonist's Guide to the Sports of the Great Outdoors*

"Wow! Look at the big one Leroy caught!"

Daniel Roberts

"I told you not to bring him!"

The Funny Side of Hunting and Fishing
A Cartoonist's Guide to the Sports of the Great Outdoors

"He must have caught a flying fish."

Daniel Roberts

"Now THAT'S what I call bait!"

The Funny Side of Hunting and Fishing
A Cartoonist's Guide to the Sports of the Great Outdoors

Daniel Roberts

*The Funny Side of Hunting and Fishing
A Cartoonist's Guide to the Sports of the Great Outdoors*

"My compliments to the chef!"

Daniel Roberts

The Funny Side of Hunting and Fishing
A Cartoonist's Guide to the Sports of the Great Outdoors

About the Author

A graphic artist and cartoonist, Daniel Roberts is a graduate of commercial art from Iowa Wesleyan College and a graduate of the Art Instruction School which he participated in during his junior and senior years of high school.

A life-long resident of the state of Iowa, he has been drawing since he tried copying the Peanuts comic strip characters at the age of four. This introduced him to his first taste of comic strip drawing. Since graduating college, he has had his cartoons published in several magazines, including *The Saturday Evening Post*, and in King Features Syndicate's *The New Breed* comic strip. Since 2000, two comic strip syndicates, Beacon Entertainment Syndicate of Tennessee and Artist Market Syndicate, have been promoting two on-going strips to newspapers.